They jump and fly and swim and crawl;
God our Father made them all.

The Standard Publishing Company, Cincinnati, Ohio
A division of Standex International Corporation
© 1994 by The Standard Publishing Company
All rights reserved.
Printed in the United States of America
01 00 99 97 96 95 94   5 4 3 2 1

Library of Congress Catalog Card Number 94-11304
ISBN 0-7847-0200-4
Cataloging-in-Publication data available
Designed by Coleen Davis

Scripture from The Bible in Today's English Version,
© 1966, 1971, 1976 by the American Bible Society.
Used by permission.

AVARICIOUS AARDVARKS

AND OTHER

Alphabet Tongue Twisters

by Sandy Sheppard
illustrated by Joel Bower

LITTLE DEER
B·O·O·K·S
PSALM 42:1

Standard Publishing
Cincinnati, Ohio

Avaricious aardvarks
antagonize
anxious ants.

Big brown baboons
buy bananas
by the bunch.

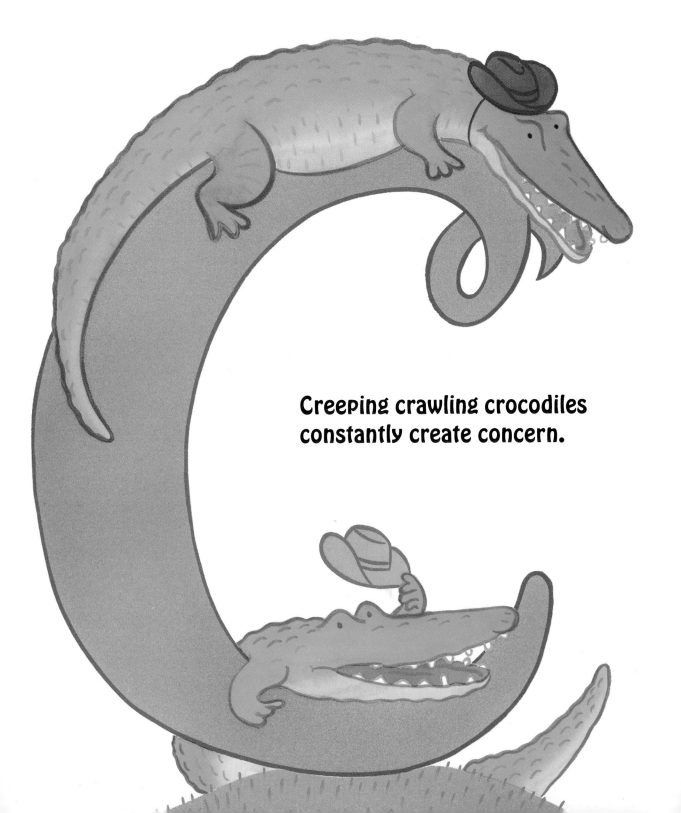

Creeping crawling crocodiles constantly create concern.

Dehydrated dromedaries don't drink daintily.

Energetic elephants enjoy exercising endlessly.

Friendly frogs frolic friskily for fun.

Gorgeous gorillas give glamorous gifts.

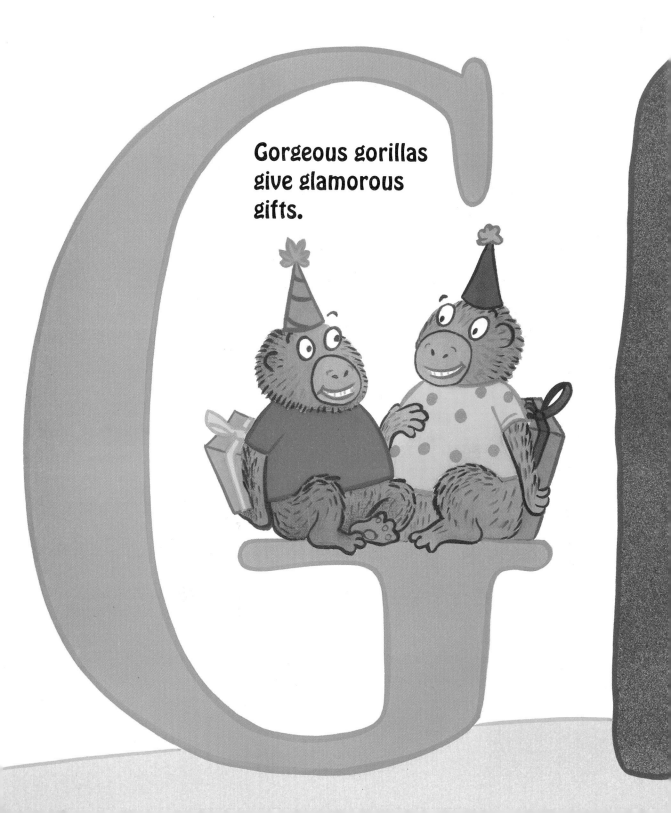

Jolly jaguars jump joyfully in jungles.

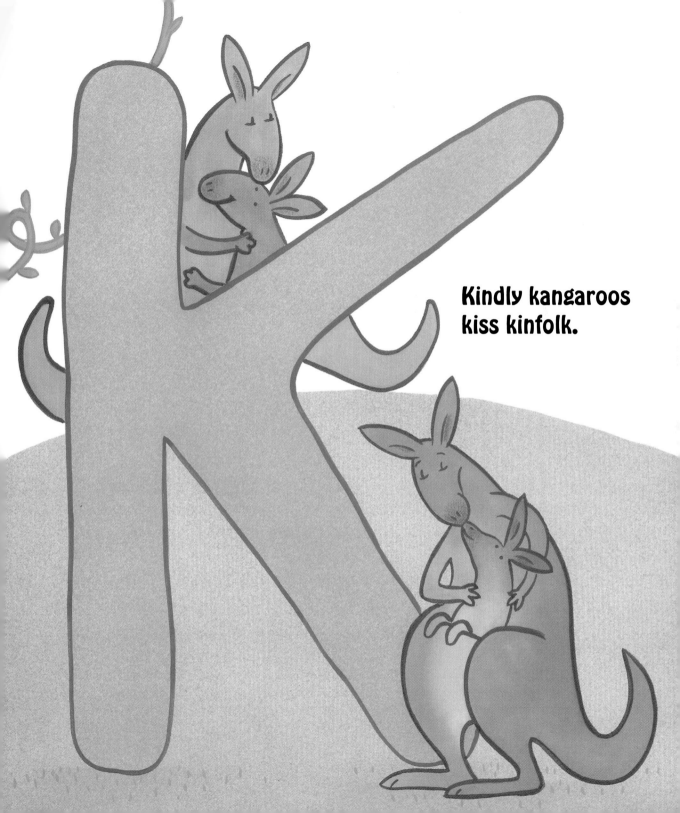

Kindly kangaroos
kiss kinfolk.

Listless lions lazily lap liquids.

Mice make mischief merrily.

Narwhals never need knitting needles.

Oodles of octopuses occupy oceans.

Perceptive poodles
prohibit petting porcupines.

Quiet quails
quaintly quilt.

Reckless rhinos
run rapidly.

Sleek seals
swiftly swallow
salmon steaks.

Terrible tigers test their trouble-making talents.

Ugly umbrella-birds
use unusual
utensils.

Venomous
vipers visit
in vivid
velvet vests.

Wealthy walruses wear waistcoats
with waterproof watches.

Extraordinary
xeruses excel
on the xylophone.

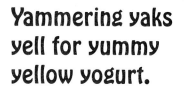

Yammering yaks yell for yummy yellow yogurt.

Zany zebras zip zigzag zippers.

Thank you, God, for your great gifts
that make us grin and giggle!

Curious beasts from A to Z
Fill the earth, the sky, the sea.